BEADS
—— in ——
TATTING

BEADS
—— in ——
TATTING

Judith Connors

Kangaroo Press

Acknowledgments

I wish to express my appreciation to:

Alison Findlay for her time in arranging and taking photographs for me

Deidre McAlister for the loan of her bobbins and for occupying Beth and William while Alison was busy, and

Betty Franks for her interest and the loan of her embroidered purse to be photographed.

First published in 1997 by Kangaroo Press Pty Ltd
3 Whitehall Road Kenthurst NSW 2156 Australia
PO Box 6125 Dural Delivery Centre NSW 2158
Printed in Hong Kong by South China Printing Co. (1988) Ltd

ISBN 0 86417 854 9

Contents

Preface 7
Introduction 8
  A brief history of beads 8
  Uses of beads 8
  Materials 13
  Shapes 14
  Methods of attachment 13
  Beads and lace 15
Beads in tatting 16
  Some useful tips 17
Symbols and abbreviations 19
Spectacles case 22
Festive snowflake 24
Decorative side comb 28
Versatile edging 30
Bridal bell 32
Beaded choker 35
Hair clasp 38
Hat band with flair 41
Daisy earrings 44
Sparkling medallion 46
Trim for a belt 50
Oops! 52
Useful references 54
Index 55

A lacemaker's prayer

Lord, let me grow old like beautiful lace,
Cherished and treasured and cared for with grace.

Anonymous

Preface

This book is designed for those who have already learnt to tat and would like to add a little 'sparkle' to their work in the way of beads. There is nothing difficult in adding beads or sequins to tatting. No special patterns are needed. All that is required is a little forward planning.

The pieces of lace in this book are introductory, but they assume that you can tat with a shuttle and are acquainted with visual patterns or diagrams, working with two shuttles, and pearl (or three-thread) tatting.

You may save time ending off in several of the patterns if you can use split rings and split chains or bridge tatting. However, these techniques are not essential.

You will be introduced to a range of techniques, some quite similar to others, but each will place beads in a different position in your lace. Some techniques require only a shuttle, others two shuttles, while the remainder need a ball thread as well.

No doubt as you make the pieces many other uses for beads will spring to mind. Try them and see the effect.

Happy creative tatting!

Judith Connors

Introduction

A brief history of beads

For thousands of years people have been fascinated by beads—for so long their origin is lost in time. They have been made from many materials and for various purposes, both utilitarian and decorative. Beads have been used as currency, for religious purposes, in numeration and as adornment, either singly or strung together. In some cultures they denoted status.

Beads were discovered in the ancient tombs of Egypt where they were used to decorate mummies. In 1922 in the tomb of Tutankhamen, flat circular beads were found on an embroidered headkerchief dating from approximately 1350 BC. In mediaeval times beads ornamented church vestments, royal robes and even armour. During the Elizabethan period semi-precious stones and jewels were sometimes sewn onto garments to prevent their theft.

The Europe of the 1800s has provided us with many examples of good decorative beading sewn by hand. Beadwork from Germany was displayed in London at the Great Exhibition of 1851. In Berlin alone at that time over 300 shades of beads were available.

By the end of the nineteenth century, beads were found almost universally and were used for diverse purposes.

Uses of beads

The uses made of beads may be classified into three broad areas:

 religious/spiritual
 decorative, and
 utilitarian.

Religious/spiritual

Because of their colours or the materials of which they are made, some beads were, and still are, considered to possess spiritual powers. Single beads are worn as talismans, while others that tinkle with movement perform a magical role in warding off evil spirits. Crystals are believed to ensure the well-being of the wearers. A set of worry beads, common in the Greek culture, is shown over the page.

Beads are important in the religious practices of Roman Catholicism, Buddhism and Hinduism. Catholics and Buddhists use beads as an aid to prayer, while Hindu devotees place strands of beads on shrines to individual gods.

Decorative

Whether singly or strung in groups, beads have adorned individual people, their garments and possessions, for thousands of years. The beads have often outlasted the fabrics to which they were attached. Discrete beads have been worn as jewellery while others have been couched or individually hand-sewn onto clothing in countless designs. Yet other beads have been woven into actual fabrics as they were manufactured.

Among the Indians of North America beaded garments indicated social status. In Europe during the thirteenth and fourteenth centuries beading added a sumptuous look to the robes of royalty and the church. So popular did beadwork become that the common people began to bead their clothes also. Eventually sumptuary laws were passed in many countries to restrict the wearing of beads to the nobility only.

During the Victorian era in Great Britain decorative beadwork was practised to excess. Encrustations of beading appeared on clothing, personal accessories and household items such as curtains, cushions, lampshades and firescreens.

As beading was done by hand, the price of elaborate work became costly. With the Industrial Revolution attempts were made to invent machines that would attach beads to fabric. This met with only limited

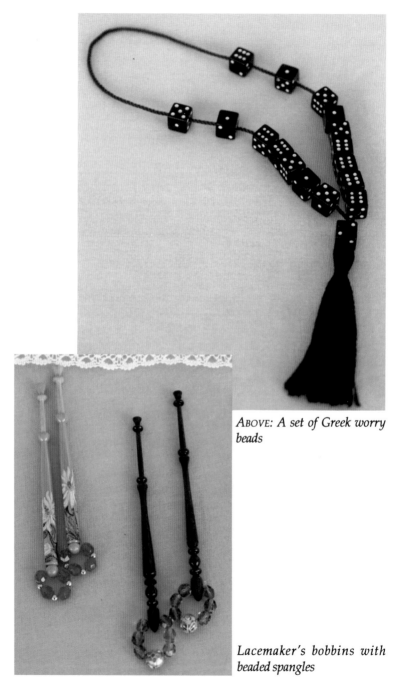

ABOVE: A set of Greek worry beads

Lacemaker's bobbins with beaded spangles

Turquoise beads set into a felt bag hand-embroidered with metallic thread

A stick pin for a lapel

success, as the machines tended to attach several beads on the one thread. As a result, even the slightest damage to a garment or other article involved the loss of several beads at a time.

Since the 1920s, the era of the flappers, beads have remained part of Western fashion, rising and falling in popularity with the style of clothing.

Utilitarian

For centuries beads have been used as articles of trade or as currency. When the Spanish ships under the leadership of Columbus reached the New World, beads were among the things offered to the native tribes there. The British and the Dutch also included beads in the goods they brought to trade with the indigenous peoples of countries they sought to colonise. Native North Americans used them as currency.

Beads threaded on a frame known as an abacus have been used for ages by the Japanese as a means of counting and reckoning. In the junior classes in many present-day schools, beads on frames are also used to teach children to count, while a frame of several columns, each with like-coloured beads, forms an apparatus for teaching place value in the Arabic numerical system.

Depending on the materials of which they were made, beads have been used as weights on the edges of food covers to prevent contamination by insects or dust. Early examples of these may be found in antique collections around the world. Other similar bead-weights are to be found on the spangles of bobbins used for lace-making. Yet others are attached to the blunt ends of hat and lapel pins to keep them in place. Here they also perform a decorative role.

Materials

Beads are made from a host of materials, some natural, others synthetic. The earliest forms of beads were probably nuts, seeds, shells, bones and teeth. Today, however, the range of materials and colours is astounding. Materials include abalone shell, amber, berries, bone, brass, clay, coral, crystal, diamond, glass, gold, horn, iron (haematite), ivory, jade, jet, lead, mother-of-pearl, nuts, oyster shell, paper, plastic, pearl, quartz, resin, scales, seeds, shells, silver, steel, stone, teeth, turquoise and wood.

While some individuals may make their own beads, renowned centres for the mass production of beads include Austria, Venice, Czechoslovakia, France, England, Germany and Japan.

Shapes

Beads come in a range of basic shapes: rocaille or seed beads, bugle beads, rice or barrel beads, round beads, teardrop beads, cut or faceted. Many other unusual shapes are also found, e.g. cubes, coins, animals.

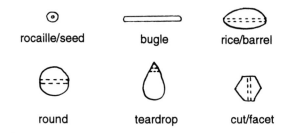

rocaille/seed   bugle   rice/barrel

round   teardrop   cut/facet

Various bead shapes

Methods of attachment

Beads may be strung singly or in groups. The earliest beads would have been strung on vines, sinews or thongs, materials which can only be assumed since the beads themselves have survived longer than the threads they were strung on. Threads employed today include wire, cotton, nylon and polyester.

Beads of crystal and haematite

Some strung beads were sewn to the edges of articles to form fringes, twists, tassels and loops, while others were couched onto fabrics following either set or free designs.

Within the cultures of some races and tribes there are traditional patterns for decorating with beads and also for threading, weaving and attaching them. These peoples pass their designs from one generation to the next. Various colours may also play significant roles.

Modern embroidered beading may be classified as hand or tambour beading. In hand-beading, the beads, or even sequins, are sewn one by one to fabric with a fine needle. In tambour or French frame beading, several beads at once are attached by means of a cornaly or hooked needle which is passed through fabric stretched over a circular frame (like a drum or tambour).

A beaded cover with a decorative looped edge

Beads and lace

Beads may also be incorporated in lacework. Some are hand-sewn to accent or highlight a section of work, as in bridal wear. Others can be added individually with the aid of a hook as lace stitches are joined together. Yet others are threaded onto ball and shuttle threads prior to the commencement of work, and then moved along into place as required, as in crochet and tatting.

Beads in tatting

It is possible to add beads in every area where tatting can be used—in furnishings, jewellery and accessories, bridal wear, Christmas decorations, photo frames and so on—and with the variety of beads available today, remarkable effects can be achieved.

At the end of the 1800s the Queen of Romania and her ladies were adding precious stones to cloths and covers they tatted for use in church ceremonies (Lady Hoare, 1910). In *The Priscilla Tatting Book No.2* (1915) there are various Victorian-style pieces of beaded work. *Tatting Patterns* (Julia E. Sanders, 1977) is an unabridged republication of this work. Rhoda Auld included an excellent range of techniques for tatting with beads in her book, *Tatting* (1974).

When you are preparing to add beads to a piece of tatting, it is wise to decide whether the beads are being used as highlights or as focal points. This will affect the sizes of the beads you choose and their placement. The weight of the thread will also influence the size, as it is not advisable to place large beads on very fine thread, nor to lose the impact of seed beads, which are very small, by using a heavy thread.

Coloured beads will add interest as well, depending on the purpose of the piece of lace. Glass beads or crystals will sparkle in the light, pearls will add a lustre.

As some beads are not regular in shape, you may need to tat a trial piece of the pattern to determine how they will lie in the proposed article. On occasions it may be necessary to change the beads you were planning to use, or to alter the pattern to suit them.

Although most modern beads are colourfast, there are some that may be affected by heat or laundering. For example, pearls and beads with an iridescent lustre may well react badly to washing. If there is any doubt, test a sample few under conditions similar to those where you intend to use them.

As beads strung on a tatting thread will occupy some space, it is advisable to use a shuttle large enough to accommodate both thread and beads. Large plastic shuttles are available at some craft retailers, but a suitable home-made one can be cut out of firm scrap plastic (e.g. milk or detergent bottles) using the pattern given below, enlarged or reduced as required. Wind the thread through the tip and around the inside prong as indicated.

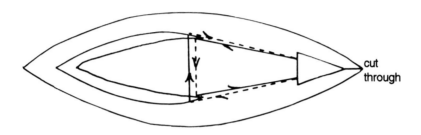

Pattern for a large shuttle

Sequins can be used in various pieces of tatting also. They are added similarly to beads but because of their different shapes and sizes will require extra planning before you include them.

Beads can be added to your tatting in five ways while you are working:

On the shuttle thread
On the ball thread
On a separate thread
Added later to formed picots
Added later to doubled shuttle or ball threads.

Adding beads and sequins will give your lace a new dimension. You will experience a sense of freedom as you create your own articles. Adventurous tatters will be limited only by their imagination.

Some useful tips

1. If you are using a lot of the same beads, add an extra one or two to the thread as you string them, just in case one breaks, or you have miscounted, or your tension is different from that of the pattern. The remaining beads may be removed when you have finished the lace.

2. It is an idea to include the beads as you wind the thread on the shuttle. This spaces them out and eliminates constantly moving them back on the spare thread as you work.

3. When you use a stiffening medium on lace with beads, always blot the beads very thoroughly to remove any residual liquid that may dull their shine or lustre.

4. Threading small beads:

(a) Thread the cotton of the shuttle through a very fine needle and then string the beads.

(b) Add a little nail varnish to the end of the cotton, when it is dry threading the beads as if using a needle.

(c) If the beads are already strung, make the first half of an overhand knot at the end of their thread, catching the shuttle thread through the knot before drawing it closed. Then slide the beads from their string, over the knot, onto the shuttle thread.

Symbols & abbreviations

Symbols

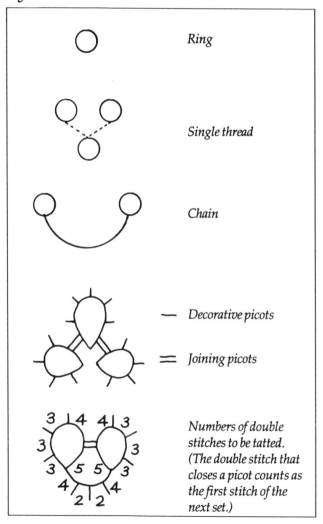

Ring

Single thread

Chain

— Decorative picots

= Joining picots

Numbers of double stitches to be tatted. (The double stitch that closes a picot counts as the first stitch of the next set.)

Abbreviations

ds = double stitch	beg = beginning
ch = chain	sh = shuttle
p = picot	prev = previous
r = ring	sp = small picot
rw = reverse work	sm = small
cl = close	lp = large picot
j = join	sep = separated

CTM = continuous thread method, i.e. do not cut the thread after winding the shuttle; this is sometimes shown as O—O when using two shuttles.

A *spacer* is a piece of card or plastic of a specific width to measure picots or spaces. If you cut your own, be sure to write its width on it for future reference.

Split ring
This is a technique developed in 1923 by Ann Orr. She called it *reverse stitch*. It was promoted later by Mary Sue Kuhn and renamed *split ring*. During the 1980s it gained in popularity and is enjoyed today by tatters all over the world because it allows you to make a series of rings end-to-end, and eliminates ending off between some rounds. See diagrams below.

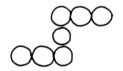

Various ring formations

The technique requires two shuttles to make a ring, one forming some of it by the normal method and the second shuttle forming reverse stitches for the other portion (see diagram). These reverse stitches are normal stitches without the transfer.

Split ring, showing two sets of stitches

Split chain

This technique is known also as *bridge tatting* or the *knotless method chain using the Dora Young loop*. In 1975 Dora Young published an ingenious series of loops which permit the tatter to progress from one round/row to the next via a bridging split chain. It eliminates ending off and is similar to the split ring in concept, but not in execution.

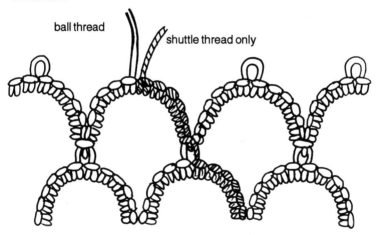

Split chains

Spectacles case

This method involves placing beads on a shuttle thread in spaces between the closed rings of a medallion. You will find it quite easy to do. The wheel pattern of the medallion was very common in the late nineteenth century.

Dimensions
Each decorative medallion has a diameter of 5 cm (2").

Materials
1 shuttle
No. 20 crochet thread
24 x 5 mm (3/16") rice or bugle beads

Put all the beads on the shuttle thread. Leave 15 cm (6") of thread before starting the inner ring. Work eleven picots, then, to form a false 12th picot, work one small split ring, i.e. do 2ds, p, 2ds normally with the shuttle, then on the other side of the ring work 2ds, p, 2ds in *reverse tatting* with the loose end. Close the ring normally. Slide one bead up beside this ring then work one large ring. Slide another bead forward. Continue the pattern, sliding up a bead between one ring and the next until the medallion is complete. End off. Make a second medallion and attach both to the case.

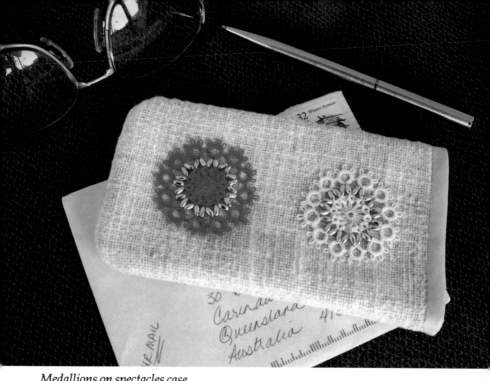

Medallions on spectacles case

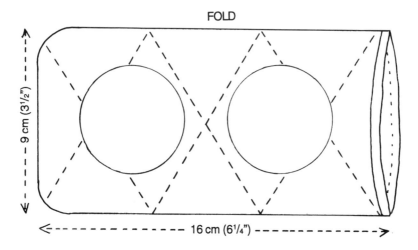

FOLD

9 cm (3¹/₂")

16 cm (6¹/₄")

Pattern for spectacles case

Plain fabric outer, felt lining, edge bound, seams machined, quilted if desired.

23

Festive snowflake

Again you will be using beads on the shuttle thread, but this time they will be included in rings as picots. Single or multiple beads may be included at each picot. It all depends on the effect you wish to create. In this pattern I have opted for single beads to add sparkle to a snowflake for your tree during the festive season.

Dimensions
Snowflake is 8 cm (3¼") across the points

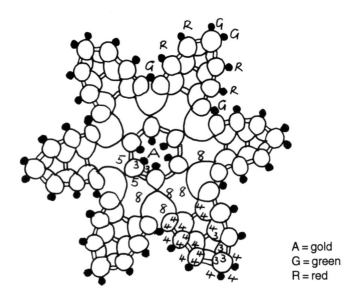

A = gold
G = green
R = red

Materials
2 shuttles
No. 40 white or silver thread
rocaille or seed beads, 6 gold, 24 red and 24 green

Christmas snowflake decoration

Threading small beads

1. Thread the cotton of the shuttle through a very fine needle and then string the beads.

2. Add a little nail varnish to the end of the cotton, when it is dry threading the beads as if using a needle.

3. If the beads are already strung, make the first half of an overhand knot at the end of their thread, catching the shuttle thread through the knot before drawing it closed. Then slide the beads from their string, over the knot, onto the shuttle thread.

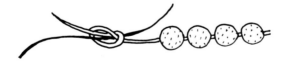

Sliding strung beads over knot

Beads that form a pattern should be threaded in *reverse order* to the way they will be added to the work, i.e. the last bead required will be threaded first. A careful study of each pattern will reveal this order.

25

For this snowflake the order of stringing is :
Shuttle 1—(2 red, 2 green, 2 red, 1 green) 6 times
Shuttle 2—6 gold

Including beads within rings

To place all these beads in the positions of picots, you will have to slide up the required number of beads *before* you start each ring and *include* it/them as you wrap the thread around your free hand prior to the first half-stitch. The bead/s will hang ready on the loop underneath. When a bead is required, slide it up over the back of your fingers into place firmly beside the last stitch (figure A). Continue tatting, making sure that the next stitch fits snugly beside the bead (figure B).

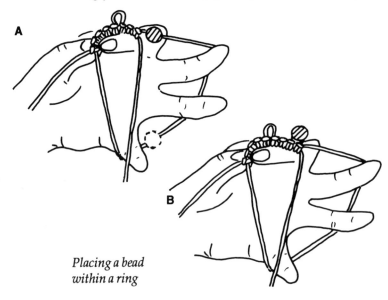

Placing a bead within a ring

Snowflake

Shuttle 2 replaces the ball thread, and also forms the rings at the centre of the piece. Thread the beads as given above, then join the two shuttle threads together.

Start with shuttle 2 to form one centre (gold) ring. Slide up one bead and include it as you wrap the thread around your hand. Work 5ds, 1p, 3ds. Move the bead into place. Continue tatting 3ds, 1p, 5ds. Close the ring. This shuttle now becomes the chain/ball thread. Using shuttle 1, chain 8ds, then continue the pattern, moving the green and red beads up as they are required.

Note

The ring at the tip of each arm of the snowflake needs 2 green beads to be moved up before you start to tat. When joining the two rings at the bottom of each V, work normally even though a green bead is already on the picot. Pass a fine crochet hook through this picot, beside the bead, and draw the shuttle thread up for normal joining. When the snowflake is complete, stiffen lightly and attach a loop as a hanger.

Stiffening mediums

1. Boil together 1 cup sugar with half a cup of water until a thick clear syrup is formed. Allow this to cool before dipping the piece into it. Blot off any excess liquid, especially on the beads. Reshape and leave to dry flat.

2. Mix well a quantity of PVA glue with water 1:1, and proceed as above.

Decorative side comb

This is yet another method where you need only a shuttle thread to produce interesting effects with beads. This time they lie across the tops of rings that form a simple braid. The beads are secured in place after the rings are closed. Rice or round beads can be used in this pattern. I have chosen rice beads here. Naturally, the larger the ring the longer or bigger the bead needs to be.

Dimensions
Side comb 9 cm (3½") wide—suitable for bridal or evening wear, or a child's communion veil.

Materials
1 shuttle
1 side comb
25 cm (10") of 10 mm (3/8") wide velvet ribbon
No. 20 cotton
8 x 5 mm (3/16") rice beads

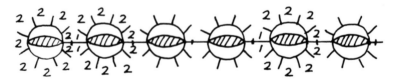

After winding the cotton on the shuttle, thread on the beads. Follow the pattern for the first ring (figure A). *After closing* the ring slide one bead up on top of it. Using a crochet hook, from the back of the 5th picot draw the thread through and secure in place to the picot by passing the shuttle through the loop formed (figure B).

It is wise to make the 5th picot a little smaller than the others to prevent the bead sliding out of place. (A long picot also tends to distort as the join is made.) Tat a second ring fairly close to the first and add a bead as before.

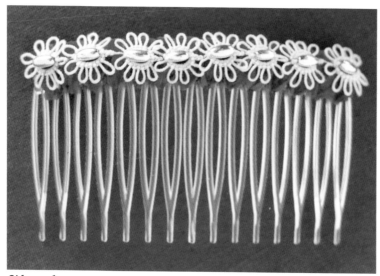

Side comb

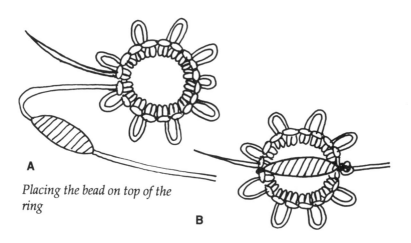

A

Placing the bead on top of the ring

B

Continue the pattern until all beads have been used or the desired length is reached.

Prepare the comb by winding the velvet ribbon around the top and between the teeth. Sew or glue the end down at the back. Carefully stitch the beaded lace in place on top of the ribbon. See page 35 for a matching choker.

METHOD 4

Versatile edging

A ball thread is introduced in this method so that chains may be tatted. The beads are placed on the ball thread and appear between sections of chain.

Dimensions
This method makes a trimming 3 cm (1¼") wide which can be of any length desired, a versatile trimming for a garment, a bag, a lampshade or a curtain tie.

Materials
1 shuttle
No. 10 cotton
10 x 10 mm (3/8") teardrop beads for each 22 cm (8¾") length of edging

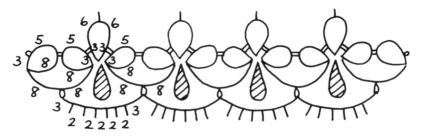

Estimate the number of beads needed for the length required, and add a few more to be on the safe side. Place the beads on the ball thread before starting to tat. Begin with the third ring of a clover and follow the pattern until the next clover is complete. Then slide up a bead beside the first chain of 8ds, p, 8ds and tat the next chain snugly beside the bead. Continue the pattern, sliding beads into the appropriate places, until the required length is reached. Continue with row 2 (which may be omitted if you wish).

Green lace with pearls

Row 1 may be worked in very fine thread with tiny teardrop beads for a dainty edging on bridal wear.

Although teardrop beads have been used in this piece of lace, any kind of bead may be used as long as it fits the space.

METHOD 5

Bridal bell

Here you will use beads on the ball thread as picots. Multiple seed beads could be used, but the bell illustrated has single seed pearls. This bell can be mounted on a cake, attached to the sides of pews or hung on a ribbon from a bride's bouquet.

Dimensions
Bridal bell 4.5 cm (1¾") high, not including the ring on the top, and 6 cm (2½") across the bottom.

Materials
2 shuttles
No. 20 cotton
18 seed pearls for the edge plus 1 seed or drop pearl for the clapper

The central ring and the first three rows at least may be worked with two shuttles CTM. Using split rings and slip-stitching from one row to the next will save joins and time.

Tat the first ring, making 8p separated by 1ds. Close the ring. Follow this by a false 9th picot formed by tatting a split ring: 2ds, p, 3ds normally and 2ds, p, 3ds of *reverse tatting*. (Refer to the medallion on the spectacles case on page 22 for the same technique.)

Note: These first nine picots should be slightly long, whereas the picots of row 1 should be quite small to accommodate all the rings neatly around the centre.

Continue the pattern as indicated. The last two rows of chain around the mouth of the bell may be done without any break in the threads, so place the 18 seed pearls onto the ball (or passive shuttle) thread before starting these rows. Follow the pattern for the first chain row. When working the last row prepare to use the pearls.

White bridal bell

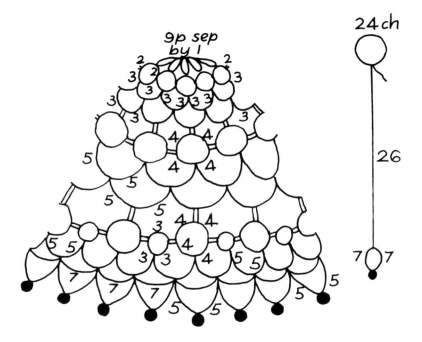

Now for each chain tat 5ds, slide a pearl up beside the last ds, then tat a further 5ds. Join the thread of shuttle 1 in the small space between each chain of 7ds and the next. Continue the pattern and end off.

If you choose, you may tat the entire bell using the split ring and split chain (bridge) techniques. In this case, the 18 seed pearls should be threaded onto shuttle 2 (chain thread) before starting.

Make the clapper of your choice, but remember to thread it through the top of the bell before forming the chain into a ring and joining. Using a lock-stitch chain for the main stem of the clapper helps keep the lace straight, whereas normal chain tends to curve a little. Stiffen the lace, reshape and leave to dry sitting on a port or sherry glass before adding ribbons, flowers or stamens.

METHOD 6

Beaded choker

In this method a second ball thread has been introduced.
Beads will be placed on both ball threads as you work a
variation on pearl tatting, also known as three-thread
tatting. This lace braid is also suitable for an Alice band.

Dimensions
A braid approximately 35 cm (14″) long.

Materials
No. 20 cotton
1 shuttle
2 ball threads of the same colour
44 x 5 mm (3/16″) rice or bugle beads for 35 cm (14″) of
    lace
40 cm (15¾″) velvet ribbon approx. 15 mm (½″–¾″) wide
small piece of double hooked tape, e.g. Velcro

Green lace on a velvet band for a choker

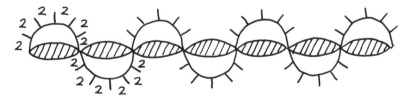

This lace is different from normal pearl tatting because
it has arched chains where there are normally loops of
thread. This is achieved by tightening the ball threads
alternately.

The choker and side comb could be made in the same colours as a matching set

Estimate the number of beads needed and place half of them on each ball thread. Join the shuttle and two ball threads together. Using one ball thread tat a chain of 2ds, 5ps separated by 2ds, 2ds, and reverse the work. Then slide up a bead on the *second* thread so that it lies beside the very first ds made. Tat a similar chain with this second thread, making sure its first ds lies right beside the last ds of the preceding chain. This should cause the first chain to arch under the bead. Reverse the work and slide up a bead on the *first* ball thread to fit snugly.

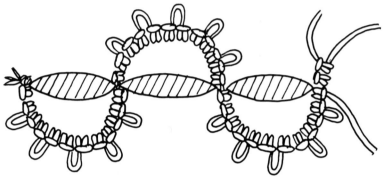

Arching chains and beads

Then continue the pattern, remembering to slide up a bead on each thread *before* tatting the respective chain (follow the diagram for guidance). Continue the lace for the required length.

Make a small hem by sewing or gluing one end of the velvet ribbon. Attach the lace to the ribbon, leave a space for the ribbon to overlap, and hem the other end. Sew one side of the hooked tape to the space just left for overlap, and the second side of the hooked tape to the other end of the ribbon.

Hair clasp

This method involves beads strung on a separate thread as well as shuttle and ball threads. The technique causes the beads to zigzag between two rows of rings on a rectangle of lace to decorate a hair clasp (or to renovate an old one).

Dimensions
Rectangular piece of lace 9 cm x 3 cm (3½" x 1¼")

Materials
1 shuttle
No. 20 thread
reel of fine gold or silver thread*
19–22 gold or silver rice or bugle beads 5 mm (3/16")
    long
1 hair clasp 9.5 cm x 3.5 cm (3¾" x 1½") with a plain
    surface

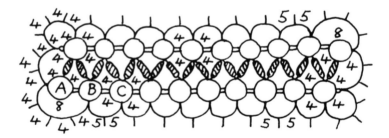

Put all the beads on a separate thread about 25 cm (10") long, leaving equal spare thread at each end. Anchor the beads loosely in place by looping one length of the spare thread over its end bead to form a half knot. Leave the other end free. Join the ball and shuttle threads. (*The fine gold or silver thread will be included here, if desired, and treated with the ball thread for *chains* only.)

Pink hair clasp

Beads zigzagging between rings

Start with the ring at the short side of the piece (4ds, join, 4ds , p, 8ds). After the first 4ds join in the free end of the bead thread, finish the ring and close. Continue the pattern to the next ring and join to the separate thread, but *leave two beads* before joining. You will find that the separate bead thread will move through the joins a little. This is useful in taking up slack and adjusting the tension. Follow the pattern for the length required, making sure there is one bead left to join to another side ring. On the return side join the rings to the thread between each pair of beads, thus forming the zigzag effect.

Remove any spare beads and sew in the ends. Attach the lace to the hair clasp, either by sewing or gluing. The gold or silver thread around the edge will catch the light and match the beads along the middle.

METHOD 8

Hat band with flair

To make this hat band you will need a shuttle and a ball thread. Loose beads will be added individually to finished picots before you make joins. The beads appear between two rings in this piece, but they could just as easily be placed between a ring and a chain, or between two chains.

Dimensions
Hat band is 58 cm (22") long, 15 mm (5/8") wide.

Materials
1 large shuttle (see pattern on page 17)
1 skein (19–20 m/21–22 yds) of rayon thread equivalent
   to No. 5–8 pearl thread
100 x 2.5 or 3 mm (1/8") beads
1 picot spacer, 11 or 13 mm (7/16" or ½"), depending on
   the beads chosen
1 crochet hook fine enough to pass through the beads

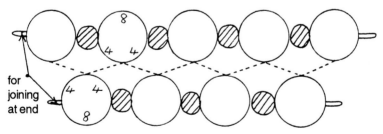

This is a simple article to tat. It will make an attractive addition to any hat. The technique involved may be applied while joining to any picot on a ring or a chain, as long as the picot is large enough to accommodate the bead.

The spacer ensures you will have a consistent length of picot to fit through the bead for joining. The first

Hat band

two rings will have two picots measured by the spacer. Each consecutive ring will need only one measured picot. The last two rings have no picots as they require two joins.

As each join is reached, place a bead on the crochet hook, catch it over the preceding picot and slide the bead onto it.

Ring and crochet hook

With the hook still in the picot, draw the thread of the working ring up through the end of the picot to form a small loop. Then pass the shuttle through the loop to make a normal join. If the beads are already strung, pass the end of their thread through the picot and back through each bead in turn as needed (see figure). Slide the bead onto the picot and withdraw the thread. Use the crochet hook to draw up the working ring as before.

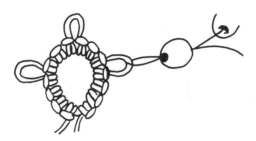

Ring and bead on thread

Continue the pattern, reversing the work and leaving a space of at least 5 mm (3/16") between rings. When the required length is reached, join (adding beads to the picots of the first two rings) and end off. Attach the band to your hat and enjoy the compliments as you wear it.

Daisy earrings

Again you will add loose beads to finished picots, but this time they will be placed across the centres of rings that are still being formed.

These earrings combine the technique used in the bridal bell on page 32 with this new technique. If you choose not to make earrings, the daisies may be used to trim anything suitable.

Dimensions
The daisies are 25 mm (1") across.

Materials
1 shuttle
No. 40 white cotton
1 fine crochet hook
7 seed beads of one colour, e.g. pearl or yellow, or 6 white and 1 yellow
1 pair earring bases, either clip-on or pierced

Put only six of the beads on the ball thread before starting. These will be moved up later as required in place of picots on the chains. Join the ball and the shuttle threads or work CTM.

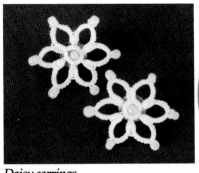

Daisy earrings

Begin tatting a ring as shown, making a special picot at least 5 mm (3/16") long when closed. It will have to reach across the closed ring. (A little practice may help.) Continue the ring until you reach the point illustrated below. Fold the long picot behind the ring, and from the front thread the seventh bead onto it with the help of the crochet hook. With the hook still in the picot, place it over the passive thread and draw this up to form a loop. Remove the crochet hook and pass the shuttle through the loop to form a stitch. Ease this gently down into place so that the shuttle thread will still run through all the stitches. Make the second half of a double stitch. Finish the ring and close. The bead should lie in the centre of the ring.

Continue the pattern of chains as petals, sliding a bead into place where indicated. Join each chain to one of the picots on the ring with the shuttle thread. When the daisy is complete, end off and stiffen. Make a second daisy to match. After they have dried attach them to earring bases with a glue gun. Vary the bead and cotton colours for different effects.

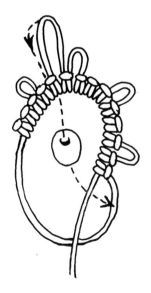

Unfinished ring with large picot and bead

45

METHOD 10

Sparkling medallion

The large bead in the middle of the central ring of this medallion involves adding a loose bead to a doubled ball thread. Other earlier methods of placing beads have been included here as well: one and two at a time on formed picots (page 41), and between chains (page 30), to create a piece which may be worn as a pendant, or used as an attractive trimming on an evening bag or on the lid of a box, for example.

Dimensions
The medallion is 6 cm (2 ³/₈")
in diameter.

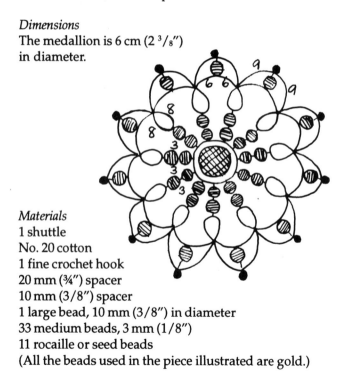

Materials
1 shuttle
No. 20 cotton
1 fine crochet hook
20 mm (¾") spacer
10 mm (3/8") spacer
1 large bead, 10 mm (3/8") in diameter
33 medium beads, 3 mm (1/8")
11 rocaille or seed beads
(All the beads used in the piece illustrated are gold.)

This whole piece may be worked CTM without a break in the thread. Before winding the shuttle (3 m/3½ yds

Pink medallion with gold beads

is plenty), thread on the 11 seed beads and 2 of the medium beads so that when you are ready to start the seed beads are on the ball side and the two medium ones are on the shuttle thread, all in reserve for later.

Begin by making a chain, but leave a loop as illustrated below. For the picots on this chain use the 20 mm (¾") spacer.

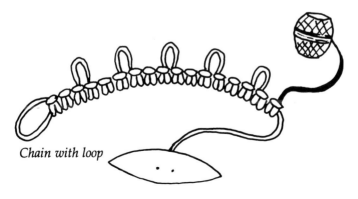

Chain with loop

This chain will become half the visible ring encircling the large bead. The loop will pass through the centre of the bead. If your bead is larger adjust the chain by adding extra *ds* in appropriate places. Now use the crochet hook to draw the loop up through the bead to make a normal join at the other end with the shuttle thread.

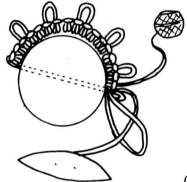

Chain halfway around bead

Make sure the tatting fits snugly against the bead. Continue the chain for the other half of the 'ring' and join to the beginning with the shuttle thread again. There should now be 10 of the eleven picots around the bead.

Slide up one medium bead from the *shuttle* thread and then chain 1ds over it. Repeat this with the second bead. This manoeuvre forms the 11th 'picot' with 2 medium beads already in place. (See note on next page for alternative method.*)

Then tat a split ring (8ds + 8ds *reverse stitch*). Work round 2 adding *two medium* beads to each of the ten remaining picots around the centre bead. Use the 10 mm

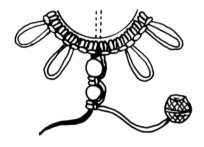

Completed ring with 2 beads

(3/8") spacer to measure the picots on the chains of round 2. Join the last chain to the base of the first (split) ring.

Round 3 is a continuous chain. Before joining, by the shuttle thread, to each picot of round 2, add one loose medium bead. Then slide up one seed bead from the ball thread and place it over the join close beside the last chain of 9ds. When joining at the base of the rings in round 2 use the shuttle thread. Complete the pattern and end off.

Add a small gold ring to an appropriate place on round 3 and thread a gold chain through it ready to wear. The medallion may be stiffened if you wish, but if all picots fit firmly through their beads, the medallion should not be floppy, and consequently will not need stiffening.

---

* *Alternative:* If you prefer that no thread shows around the beads, do not follow this manoeuvre. Simply cut both the ball and the shuttle threads leaving 8–10 cm (3"–4") ends. Do not end off. Start round 2 at any picot around the centre bead and work it in its entirety. When you come to the ring matching the loose ends on the centre bead, make a very small picot and continue tatting right to the end of round 3. Then thread both the loose ends of the centre through two medium beads, draw one of the ends through the very small picot, tie both threads together and end off.

Trim for a belt

Here is another method with beads on a separate thread. This time they are large flat ones with holes from side to side. You will need two larger shuttles, each containing at least twice the length of the lace required. Chain arches are tatted around the beads, first on one side, then on the other. To maintain a good tension it is better to proceed one bead at a time, completing both arches before working the next bead. Joins to the separate thread are made with shuttle threads. Different coloured threads may be used on opposite sides, as in the example illustrated, or you can work in one colour.

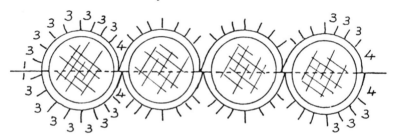

Arched chains around beads

This piece was tatted in rayon thread, which would be equivalent to a No. 5–8 pearl cotton. The beads are 20 mm (¾") in diameter. The finished tatting was attached to a tailored fabric belt. This type of trimming could also be attached to the strap of a bag or purse, or to a wall hanging.

Tatted trims on hat and belts

Detail of belt trim with large flat silver beads

Oops!

METHOD 12

There may come a time when you are tatting a ring that you discover you have forgotten to include a bead ready for placement at a picot (as in Method 2 on page 24). Don't despair! In this case, there are two alternatives.

The first one is to unpick the work and start the ring again. The second is to slide the bead up from the shuttle thread and to tat over it.

Bead with thread across it

You will notice, however, that this leaves a thread lying across the bead. Depending on the nature of your piece of lace, this may go undetected. The choice is yours.

METHOD 13

On another occasion you may have used all the beads that you threaded, but still need one more for either a ring or a chain. This can be solved by making a fold in the passive thread to form a loop. Catch the loop down through a loose bead and then pass the shuttle through the exposed loop (see page 53). Ease the bead and the loop down into place, making sure that the shuttle thread still runs freely through the stitches. Make the second half of a double stitch and continue the pattern.

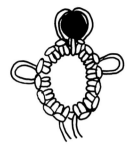

*Bead with loop through
the middle*

The bead will have threads encasing it, which under certain conditions may be attractive. A whole piece of lace may be tatted this way for the effect.

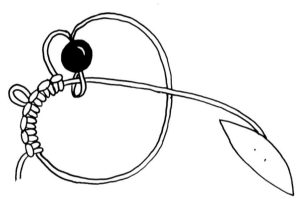

Passing the shuttle through the loop

Useful references

Auld, Rhoda: *Tatting*, Van Nostrand Rheinhold, New York, 1974 edition

Dyer, Anne: *To Boldly Go Where No Shuttle Has Gone Before*, Point Ground, Denver, CO, 1995 edition

Helm, Alice: *Bridal Tatting*, DMC, NJ, 1992 edition

Hoare, Lady: *The Art of Tatting*, Lacis Publications, Berkeley, CA, 1982 edition

Haan-van Beek, To De: *New Dimensions in Tatting*, Lacis Publications, Berkeley, CA, 1994 edition

Ikuta, Mituko: *Tatting and Bead Tatting 1*, Japan Publications, 1994 edition

Ikuta, Mituko: *Tatting and Bead Tatting 2*, Japan Publications, 1995 edition

Jones, Rebecca: *The Complete Book of Tatting*, Lacis Publications, Berkeley, CA, 1992 edition

Konior, Mary: *Tatting in Lace*, Kangaroo Press, Sydney, 1988 edition

Konior, Mary: *Tatting Patterns*, B.T. Batsford, London, 1989 edition

Konior, Mary: *Tatting with Visual Patterns*, Lacis Publications, Berkeley, CA, 1992 edition

Nicholls, Elgiva: *Tatting: Technique and History*, Dover Publications, New York, 1984 edition

Sanders, Julia E.: *Tatting Patterns*, Dover Publications, New York, 1977 edition

Sparks, Phyllis: Practical Tatting, Lacis Publications, Berkeley, CA, 1994 edition

Waller, Irene: *Tatting: A Contemporary Art Form*, Studio Vista, London, 1974 edition

Index

Abbreviations, 20
Attaching beads, 9, 14

Beaded choker, 35, 36
Beads
    across rings, 28, 29
    and lace, 15
    as picots, 24, 25, 32, 33, 44, 45, 52
    as centres of rings, 44-7
    between chains, 30, 31, 46
    between rings, 22, 23
    in tatting, 16
    on ball thread, 30, 32, 35, 44, 47
    on chains, 32
    on formed picots, 41-9
    on loops, 46, 52
    on separate threads, 38, 40, 50
    on shuttle thread, 22, 24, 28, 47
    within rings, 24-7
Bridal bell, 32, 33
Bridge tatting, 7, 21, 34

Colours, 8, 9, 14, 16
Continuous thread method (CTM), 20, 32, 44, 46

Daisy earrings, 44, 45
Decorative side comb, 28, 29
Double shuttle tatting (see Two shuttles)

Edgings, 14, 15, 30, 31

Festive snowflake, 24, 25

Hair clasp, 38, 39
Hand-beading, 9, 14, 15
Hat band with flair, 41, 42
History of beads, 8

Knotless method chain, 21

Large shuttle, 17, 41, 50

Materials, 13
Medallions, 22, 23, 46, 47
Mistakes, 52

Order of beads, 25

Pearl tatting, 7, 35, 36
Prestrung beads, 25, 43

Reverse stitch, 20-2, 32, 48

Sequins, 7, 17
Shapes of beads, 13, 16
Spacer, 20, 41, 46
Sparkling medallion, 46, 47
Spectacles case, 22, 23
Split chain, 7, 21, 34
Split ring, 7, 20, 21, 34
Stiffening mediums, 27
Symbols, 19

Tambour beading, 14
Threading small beads, 18, 25
Three thread tatting, 7, 35, 36
Trim for a belt, 50, 51
Two shuttles, 7, 20, 21, 24, 32, 50

Useful tips, 17
Uses of beads
    decorative, 9
    religious, 9
    utilitarian, 12

Using a crochet hook, 27, 28, 42, 45, 48

Versatile edging, 30, 31

Ways of adding beads, 17